ADVENTURES

How to Use Your SD-X Reader with This Book

This highly interactive book lets you explore the world in an interactive format. You can read the book and study the maps, photographs, and illustrations, but a touch of the SD-X Reader adds in-depth audio information, word definitions, and learning games to the pictures and maps.

1. Press the Power button to turn the SD-X Reader on or off. The LED will light up when the SD-X Reader is on.

2. Touch the volume buttons found on this page or on the Table of Contents page to adjust the volume.

3. Touch photographs, maps, and illustrations with the SD-X Reader to hear additional information. In a block of text, touch words that are a different color or size to hear a definition or more information.

4. As you touch around the page, you'll encounter games and quizzes. Touch the header or image that started the game to stop playing the game.

5. After two minutes of inactivity, the Reader will beep and go to sleep.

6. If the batteries are low, the Reader will beep twice and the LED will start blinking. Replace the batteries by following the instructions on the next page. The SD-X Reader uses two AAA batteries.

7. To use headphones or earbuds, plug them into the headphone jack on the bottom of the SD-X Reader.

CHANGE THE VOLUME WITH THESE BUTTONS

UP

DOWN

Battery Information
Interactive Pen includes 2 replaceable AAA batteries (UM-4 or LR03).

Battery Installation
1. Open battery door with small flat-head or Phillips screwdriver.
2. Install new batteries according to +/- polarity. If batteries are not installed properly, the device will not function.
3. Replace battery door; secure with small screw.

Battery Safety
Batteries must be replaced by adults only. Properly dispose of used batteries. Do not dispose of batteries in fire; batteries may explode or leak. See battery manufacturer for disposal recommendations. Do not mix alkaline, standard (carbon-zinc), or rechargeable (nickel-cadmium) batteries. Do not mix old and new batteries. Only recommended batteries of the same or equivalent type should be used. Remove weakened or dead batteries. Never short-circuit the supply terminals. Non-rechargeable batteries are not to be recharged. Do not use rechargeable batteries. If batteries are swallowed, in the USA, promptly see a doctor and have the doctor phone 1-202-625-3333 collect. In other countries, have the doctor call your local poison control center. Batteries should be changed when sounds mix, distort, or become otherwise unintelligible as batteries weaken. The electrostatic discharge may interfere with the sound module. If this occurs, please simply restart the product.

In Europe, the dustbin symbol indicates that batteries, rechargeable batteries, button cells, battery packs, and similar materials must not be discarded in household waste. Batteries containing hazardous substances are harmful to the environment and to health. Please help to protect the environment from health risks by telling your children to dispose of batteries properly and by taking batteries to local collection points. Batteries handled in this manner are safely recycled.

Warning: Changes or modifications to this unit not expressly approved by the party responsible for compliance could void the user's authority to operate the equipment.

NOTE: This equipment has been tested and found to comply with the limits for a Class B digital device, pursuant to Part 15 of the FCC Rules. These limits are designed to provide reasonable protection against harmful interference in a residential installation. This equipment generates, uses, and can radiate radio frequency energy and, if not installed and used in accordance with the instructions, may cause harmful interference to radio communications. However, there is no guarantee that interference will not occur in a particular installation. If this equipment does cause harmful interference to radio or television reception, which can be determined by turning the equipment off and on, the user is encouraged to try to correct the interference by one or more of the following measures: Reorient or relocate the receiving antenna. Increase the separation between the equipment and receiver. Connect the equipment into an outlet on a circuit different from that to which the receiver is connected. Consult the dealer or an experienced radio TV technician for help.

Cover art from Shutterstock.com.

Interior art from Encyclopædia Britannica, Inc. and Shutterstock.com. Select art from Library of Congress Prints and Photographs Division (5, 56, 57); NASA/JSC (58, 59); NASA/KSC (59).

Louis Weber, CEO
Publications International, Ltd.
7373 North Cicero Avenue
Lincolnwood, Illinois 60712

Permission is never granted for commercial purposes.

Publications International, Ltd.

Customer Service
customer_service@pubint.com

IISBN: 978-1-4508-8410-5

Manufactured in China.

8 7 6 5 4 3 2 1

CONTENTS

CHANGE THE VOLUME WITH THESE BUTTONS

UP

DOWN

INTRODUCTION

People travel for many different reasons. When people travel for pleasure they are called tourists. People have been traveling for pleasure at least since Roman times, when rich tourists traveled to the Italian coast for holidays. Pilgrimages, or journeys to places of religious importance, are early examples of tourism that are still popular today.

WHAT DO YOU KNOW?

YES

NO

More than half of the world's geysers can be found in Yellowstone National Park.

NATIONAL PARKS

A national park may be set aside for purposes of public recreation and enjoyment or because of its historical or scientific interest. The national parks in the United States and Canada tend to focus on the protection of both land and wildlife, those in Great Britain focus mainly on the land, and those in Africa primarily exist to conserve animals.

WORLD HERITAGE SITES

World Heritage sites are areas or objects located throughout the world that have been designated as having "outstanding universal value." Because of their value, they have been placed on the United Nations Educational, Scientific and Cultural Organization (UNESCO) World Heritage List to be preserved and protected. World Heritage designations often encourage tourism.

Palace of Versailles

Pyramids of Giza

THERE ARE THREE TYPES OF WORLD HERITAGE SITES:

- CULTURAL SITES
- NATURAL SITES
- MIXED SITES

FAMOUS TRAVELERS

The urge to travel is as old as civilization. The great historian Herodotus roamed the ancient world, examining the customs of many lands. In the AD 1200s Marco Polo traveled from Europe to Asia. Ibn Battutah traveled about 75,000 miles (121,000 kilometers) in the AD 1300s and described his experiences in a famous travel book called the *Rihlah* (*Travels*). Many other great travelers followed.

CAPTAIN JAMES COOK FRS

790F 2009
MARCO POLO
RWANDA

THE AGE OF EUROPEAN EXPLORATION

A great age of European exploration by sea began in the 1400s. Portuguese explorers sailed along the coasts of Africa, Arabia, and India. In 1492, Christopher Columbus sailed west and landed in the Americas. Sailing for England, John Cabot reached the north coast of North America in 1497. In 1500, Spanish explorer Vicente Pinzón landed in Brazil. In the same year Pedro Álvares Cabral, a Portuguese navigator, also landed there. Vasco Nuñez de Balboa of Spain crossed the Isthmus of Panama and found the Pacific Ocean in 1513. Shortly thereafter the Spaniard Hernán Cortés conquered and explored Mexico. In 1522, Ferdinand Magellan's ship completed the first voyage around the world. In the 1530s the Spaniard Francisco Pizarro conquered and explored Peru. In 1542 Juan Cabrillo explored the California coast for Spain. Also during the first half of the 16th century the Spanish conquerors Hernando de Soto and Francisco Coronado, seeking gold in North America, covered great stretches of land unknown to Europeans.

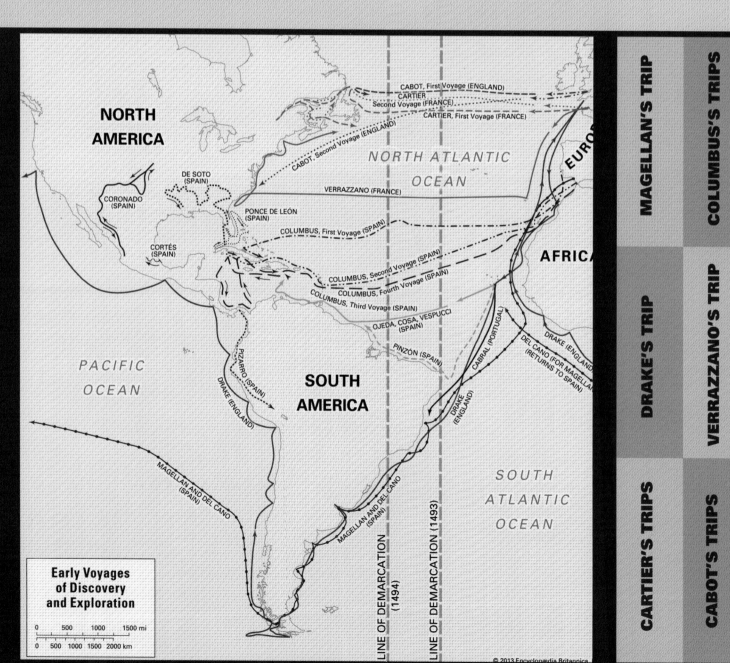

Early Voyages of Discovery and Exploration

0   500   1000   1500 mi

0   500 1000 1500 2000 km

MAGELLAN'S TRIP

COLUMBUS'S TRIPS

DRAKE'S TRIP

VERRAZZANO'S TRIP

CARTIER'S TRIPS

CABOT'S TRIPS

© 2013 Encyclopædia Britannica

TOOLS OF THE TRADE

When European exploration by sea began in the 1400s, several instruments, including the astrolabe and, later, the sextant and chronometers, or timekeeping devices, made travel by sea possible. They allowed sailors to figure out where they were and to follow a course while on the open sea.

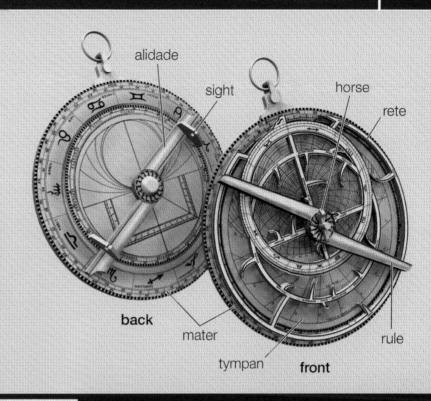

alidade

sight

horse

rete

back

mater

tympan

front

rule

HENRY THE NAVIGATOR

It was not until the days of Prince Henry of Portugal that the Age of Discovery began. Within about 30 years of Henry the Navigator's death in 1460, Europeans had explored the east coasts of the Americas, from Greenland to Cape Horn. European explorers had also visited the coasts of eastern Africa, Arabia, Persia, and India and had discovered numerous islands in the Indian Ocean.

EUROPEAN EXPLORERS

FRANCIS DRAKE

JOHN CABOT

BARTOLOMEU DIAS

JACQUES CARTIER

VICENTE PINZÓN

CHRISTOPHER COLUMBUS

FERDINAND MAGELLAN

EXPLORING N

Champlain's Explorations

- ·—·—·→ 1603
- ——→ 1604
- ·········→ 1609
- ----→ 1615-16

St. Lawrence River

Quebec

Ottawa R.

Lake Champlain

L. Huron

L. Erie

L. Ontario

Cape Cod

ATLANTIC OCEAN

© 2010 EB, Inc.

The French explorer Samuel de Champlain traveled along the seacoasts, lakes, and rivers of North America in the early 1600s. Known as the Father of New France, he founded the city of Quebec and encouraged French settlement in what is now Canada.

PACIFIC OCEAN

Fort Clatsop

S
T

← Rout

← Retu

o Note

The French explorer René-Robert Cavelier, sieur (lord) de La Salle, was the first European to travel down the Mississippi River to the Gulf of Mexico.

TRUE OR FALSE?

T   **F**

Statue of French explorer René-Robert Cavelier, sieur (lord) de La Salle, in Baton Rouge, Louisiana

RTH AMERICA

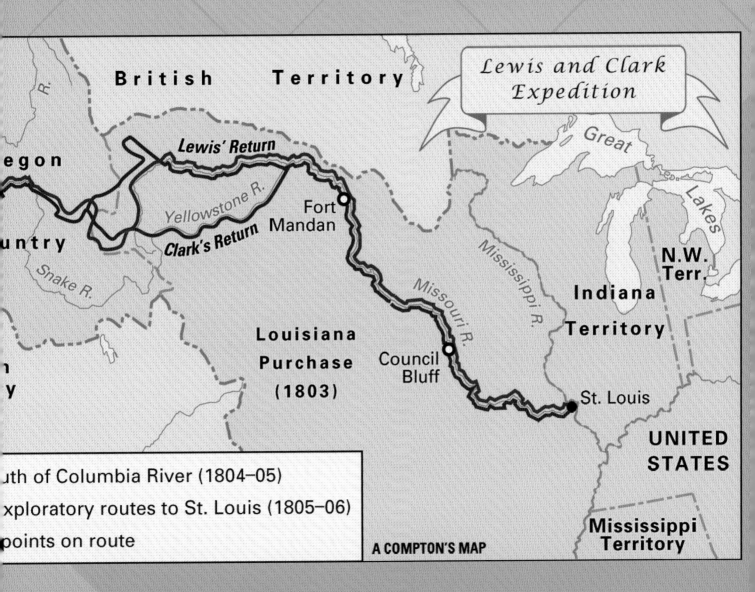

British Territory

Lewis and Clark Expedition

Great Lakes

Oregon

Lewis' Return

Yellowstone R.

Fort Mandan

Clark's Return

Mississippi R.

N.W. Terr.

Snake R.

Indiana Territory

Missouri R.

Louisiana Purchase (1803)

Council Bluff

St. Louis

UNITED STATES

uth of Columbia River (1804–05)

xploratory routes to St. Louis (1805–06)

points on route

A COMPTON'S MAP

Mississippi Territory

In 1804–06 U.S. President Thomas Jefferson sent an expedition, led by Meriwether Lewis and William Clark, to explore the North American continent from Missouri west to the Pacific Ocean—largely territory that had just been acquired in the Louisiana Purchase.

CHRISTOPHER COLUMBUS WAS NOT THE FIRST EUROPEAN TO REACH THE NORTH AMERICAN CONTINENT. DO YOU KNOW WHO WAS?

HISTORIC JOURNEYS IN NORTH AMERICA

OREGON TRAIL

In the mid- to late-1800s, thousands of U.S. pioneers traveled west on the Oregon Trail. The trail ran from Independence, Missouri, to what is now northern Oregon, near the Columbia River. It was about 2,000 miles (3,200 kilometers) long. Pioneers traveled the Oregon Trail in covered wagons pulled by horses, mules, or oxen. For safety, many wagons joined together in lines called wagon trains. Wagon trains first used the trail in the early 1840s. In the 1860s railroads began replacing much of the travel by wagon train.

The Oregon Trail followed paths that had already been discovered. Between 1804 and 1806 the explorers Meriwether Lewis and William Clark traveled from Missouri to Oregon and back. Fur traders and missionaries later found other paths that became part of the trail.

Many of the loaded covered wagons weighed between 3,000 and 7,000 pounds (1,360 and 3,175 kilograms).

BY THE NUMBERS

1842
1,400
875
2,700
1,000
1869
2,000

HOW LONG DID THE TRIP TO OREGON TAKE?

Map

ROCKY MOUNTAINS

Cascade Mountains

Snake River

South Pass

Great Salt Lake

Colorado River

Santa Fe

Red River of the North

North Platte River

Missouri River

Fort Laramie

Fort Kearny

Independence

Arkansas River

Great Lakes

Ohio River

Mississippi River

Rio Grande

ATLANTIC OCEAN

PACIFIC OCEAN

Gulf of Mexico

0   200   400 miles
0   200   400 kilometers

N
W   E
S

Legend:
← Oregon Trail
— Modern boundary
⊐ Fort
⋈ Pass

© 2012 Encyclopædia Britannica, Inc.

WHO WERE THE CONDUCTORS?

TRANSCONTINENTAL RAILROAD

The first railroads in the United States connected cities on the East Coast. In the 1850s the tracks were extended to reach cities to the west. In 1862 the U.S. government paid two railroad companies to complete a route from the Missouri River to California. The Central Pacific began laying track eastward from Sacramento, California, in 1863. The Union Pacific started westward from Omaha, Nebraska, two years later. They met in Promontory, Utah, on May 10, 1869. The transcontinental railroad opened up the country to travelers as well as companies that wanted an easy way to ship their goods.

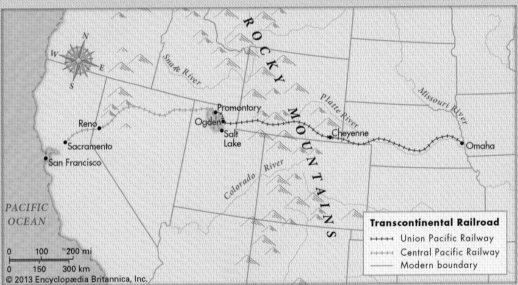

© 2013 Encyclopædia Britannica, Inc.

UNDERGROUND RAILROAD

The Underground Railroad was a secret organization that helped escaped slaves from the South reach places of safety in the North or in Canada. The Underground Railroad had to be secret because it was against the law. Laws called the Fugitive Slave acts protected slaveholders' rights even in states that did not allow slavery. The people who ran the Underground Railroad were abolitionists. They wanted to end slavery in all states.

The Underground Railroad used railway terms as code words. The routes to freedom were called "lines." The hiding places on the lines were called "stations." The people who moved or hid the slaves were called "conductors." The slaves themselves were sometimes called "freight." Estimates of the number of slaves who "rode" the Underground Railroad range from 40,000 to 100,000. The Railroad's activities ended with the beginning of the Civil War in 1861.

DISCOVER NORTH AMERICA

The CN Tower, also called the Canadian National Tower, is a broadcast and telecommunications tower in Toronto. Standing at a height of 1,815 feet (553 meters), it was the world's tallest freestanding structure until 2007, when it was surpassed by a building in Dubai, United Arab Emirates. The CN Tower is a major tourist attraction that includes observation decks, a revolving restaurant at some 1,151 feet (351 meters), and an entertainment complex.

In western Honduras, near the border with Guatemala, lies a ruined ancient Maya city named Copán. The site's many standing stone slabs, called stelae or steles, are carved with portrait sculptures and with Maya hieroglyphics (writing using pictures as symbols). The Hieroglyphic Stairway, which leads to one of the temples, is beautifully carved with some 1,260 hieroglyphic symbols. There is evidence that astronomers in Copán calculated the most accurate solar calendar produced by the Maya up to that time.

The Golden Gate Bridge is a famous landmark in northern California. The bridge spans the Golden Gate, which is the narrow body of water between San Francisco Bay and the Pacific Ocean. Despite its name, the bridge is painted a reddish orange, not gold. The bright color is called "international orange."

THE GATEWAY ARCH SWAYS UP TO 1 INCH (2.5 CENTIMETERS) IN 20-MILE- (32-KILOMETER-) PER-HOUR WINDS.

BY THE NUMBERS

1,260

189

4,200

630

1,815

354

Clear, warm water, spectacular coral reefs, and abundant marine life make Cozumel, Mexico, one of the world's best scuba-diving destinations as well as a major resort. Cozumel is an island in the Caribbean Sea, about 10 miles (16 kilometers) off the eastern coast of the Yucatán Peninsula, in southeastern Mexico. Measuring about 29 miles (46 kilometers) from northeast to southwest and averaging 9 miles (14 kilometers) in width, it is the largest of Mexico's inhabited islands.

Since 1886 the Statue of Liberty has stood in New York Bay as a symbol of the United States. The majestic sculpture is one of the largest statues ever built. With its concrete base, the structure stands 305 feet (93 meters) high. Visitors can climb the 354 steps from the base of the pedestal to the head of the Statue of Liberty.

The Gateway Arch is a towering steel structure standing on the west bank of the Mississippi River in St. Louis, Missouri. The arch is 630 feet (192 meters) tall. The distance between its two legs is equal to its height. Visitors can ride a tram up to the top for views of the city, river, and surrounding land.

North America's National Parks

MESA VERDE NATIONAL PARK

Location: Colorado, U.S.
Established: 1906
Area: 81 square miles
(210 square kilometers)
Features: The park preserves a large complex of cliff dwellings that were built hundreds of years ago by the Ancestral Pueblo (Anasazi) people. Visitors can tour some of the ruins, including the Cliff Palace. There are also hiking trails and a museum that teaches about the history of the area and the life of the Ancestral Pueblo people.

WHAT DOES THE NAME MESA VERDE MEAN?

DENALI NATIONAL PARK AND PRESERVE

Location: Alaska, U.S.
Established: 1917
Area: 7,408 square miles
(19,187 square kilometers)
Features: The park and preserve encompass the heart of the rugged Alaska Range. It combines the former Mount McKinley National Park and the Denali National Monument. Central to the park is Mount McKinley (Denali). Other highlights of the park include the large glaciers of the Alaska Range, Mount Foraker, the Savage River area, and the region's pristine environment. Wildlife is abundant in the park and preserve. Large mammals include moose, brown (grizzly) and black bears, wolves, caribou, and Dall sheep.

RECORD HOLDERS

YELLOWSTONE	YOSEMITE
DENALI	EVERGLADES
BANFF	

How did Mount McKinley get its name?

Cliff Palace

Dall sheep in Denali

Mount McKinley (also called Denali) rises to a height of 20,320 feet (6,194 meters). The mountain is scaled by hundreds of climbers each year

YOSEMITE NATIONAL PARK

Location: California, U.S

Established: 1890

Area: 1,169 square miles (3,028 square kilometers)

Features: Situated in the heart of the Sierra Nevada mountain range, the park is known for its imposing granite mountains and for its many waterfalls. Thousands of people come to Yosemite every year to camp, bike, and hike the park's many trails. Many of the most popular sites are in Yosemite Valley.

Yosemite Valley

Yosemite Falls

BANFF NATIONAL PARK

Location: Alberta, Canada

Established: 1887

Area: 2,564 square miles (6,641 square kilometers)

Features: Banff National Park is a scenic natural and wilderness area noted for its beauty, plant and animal diversity, and ongoing geologic processes. The park is also noted for its stunning alpine lakes, particularly Lake Louise, stretching northeastward from Mount Columbia, and, a short distance to the south, Moraine Lake.

Gondola ride in Banff National Park

Lake Louise

EVERGLADES NATIONAL PARK

Location: Florida, U.S.

Established: 1947

Area: 2,357 square miles (6,105 square kilometers)

Features: Everglades National Park preserves a unique blend of temperate and tropical species and freshwater and marine habitats. Several visitor centers have natural history exhibits. The park is popular with boating and canoeing enthusiasts. There are several marked canoe trails, including the 99-mile (159-kilometer) Wilderness Waterway along the park's western side.

Alligators in Everglades National Park

WHO COINED THE TERM *BADLAND*?

Badlands National Park, South Dakota, U.S.

ROAD TRIP
NORTH AMERICA

The Spanish built the first roads in North America along Native American trails. Early roads in colonial America were usually dirt, sometimes covered with rows of logs. As cars became popular in the early 1900s, people began building more roads paved with concrete and asphalt. In the 1950s the United States began building a system of large roads, called highways, across the country.

TRANS-CANADA HIGHWAY

A monument in Victoria on Vancouver Island, British Columbia, marks mile zero.

Wigwam Village Motel #6

Cadillac Ranch

ROUTE 66

Route 66 was one of the first national highways for motor vehicles in the United States and one that became an icon in American popular culture. The highway ran from Chicago, Illinois, to Los Angeles, California. From east to west, the route passed through the states of Illinois, Missouri, Kansas (only for a few miles), Oklahoma, Texas, New Mexico, Arizona, and California.

Alaska Highway

Pan-American Highway

Blue Ridge Parkway

There are about 120 million miles (193 million kilometers) of roads in the world. The United States has the largest road network, with more than 4 million miles (6 million kilometers) of roads and streets.

WHICH HIGHWAY?

EARLY EXPLORATION OF SOUTH AMERICA

TOUCH A CITY ON THE MAP TO LEARN ABOUT IT.

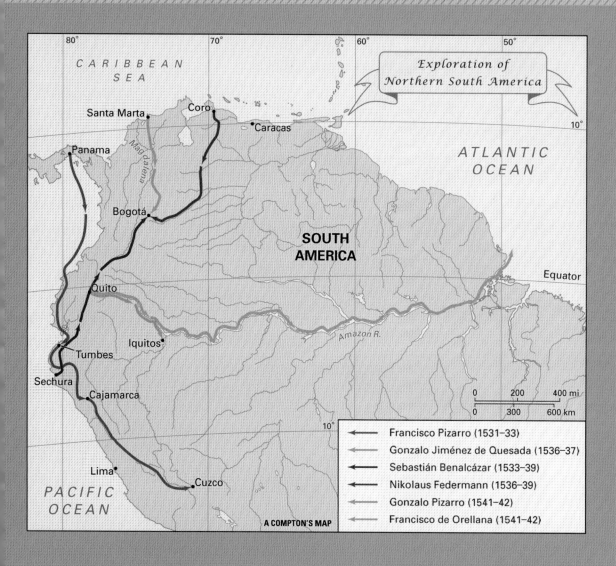

Exploration of Northern South America

Route	Explorer
→	Francisco Pizarro (1531–33)
→	Gonzalo Jiménez de Quesada (1536–37)
→	Sebastián Benalcázar (1533–39)
→	Nikolaus Federmann (1536–39)
→	Gonzalo Pizarro (1541–42)
→	Francisco de Orellana (1541–42)

A COMPTON'S MAP

THE SEARCH FOR FABLED RICHES

Much of the drive to explore and conquer northern South America came from tales of Eldorado—either a fantastically wealthy Indian ruler or a land filled with gold. In the 1530s three expeditions searching for this legendary source of riches arrived in New Granada (now Colombia) from different directions. The leaders of these expeditions were Gonzalo Jiménez de Quesada and Sebastián de Benalcázar of Spain and Nikolaus Federmann of Germany.

HOW DID THE AMAZON RIVER GET ITS NAME?

PIZARRO CONQUERS
THE INCA OF PERU

In 1523, hearing of a vast and wealthy Indian empire in South America, Francisco Pizarro enlisted the help of two friends—a soldier, Diego de Almagro, and a priest, Hernando de Luque—to form an expedition to explore and conquer the land. Early expeditions failed, but in 1531 he reached the lands of the Inca in what is now Peru. Pizarro and his men entered the Inca city of Cajamarca on November 15, 1531. With better weapons, the Spaniards easily defeated the Inca. They took gold and silver from the Inca and killed their emperor, Atahuallpa. Pizarro went on to take control of all Peru.

FRANCISCO PIZARRO

EXPLORERS QUIZ

GONZALO JIMÉNEZ DE QUESADA

DIEGO DE ALMAGRO

FRANCISCO PIZARRO

FRANCISCO DE ORELLANA

SEBASTIÁN DE BENALCÁZAR

GONZALO PIZARRO

ORELLANA EXPLORES THE AMAZON

When Francisco Pizarro's half brother, Gonzalo, prepared an expedition to explore the regions east of Quito, Francisco de Orellana was appointed his lieutenant. In April 1541 he was sent ahead of the main party to seek provisions, taking 50 soldiers. He reached the junction of the Napo and Marañón rivers, where he was persuaded of the impossibility of returning to Pizarro. Instead, Orellana became the first European to explore the course of the Amazon River.

80 CTS

FRANCISCO DE ORELLANA

CORREOS

ESPAÑA

1965 F.N.M.T.

FRANCISCO DE ORELLANA

SCIENTIFIC EXPLORATION OF

SOUTH AMERICA

The first European expeditions explored South America mainly to conquer it and to amass wealth. Missionaries who wanted to convert the Indians to Christianity also traversed the continent. In the 18th and 19th centuries many scientific explorers arrived in South America to study its geography, peoples, plants, and animals.

HUMBOLDT AND BONPLAND

In 1799 German naturalist and explorer Alexander von Humboldt set sail from France accompanied by French botanist Aimé Bonpland. Humboldt and Bonpland spent five years, from 1799 to 1804, in Central and South America. They covered more than 6,000 miles (9,650 kilometers) on foot, on horseback, and in canoes. Humboldt and Bonpland returned with a collection of several thousand new plants as well as data on longitudes and latitudes, measurements of Earth's geomagnetic field, and daily weather observations. Humboldt published 30 volumes containing the expedition's scientific results.

Orinoco River

EXPLORING THE ANDES

Humboldt and Bonpland made an extensive exploration of the Andes. From Bogotá, Colombia, to Trujillo, Peru, they wandered over the Andean Highlands. They climbed a number of peaks, including all the volcanoes around Quito, Ecuador. Humboldt's ascent of Chimborazo to a height of 19,286 feet (5,878 meters), but short of the summit, remained a world mountain-climbing record for nearly 30 years.

RISING TO 20,702 FEET (6,310 METERS), CHIMBORAZO IS THE HIGHEST PEAK IN ECUADOR.

Alexander von Humboldt

CHARLES DARWIN

In the 18th century the British navy sent a series of expeditions to chart the coastlines of South America. Naturalists began to join these expeditions, which provided unique opportunities to study the natural histories of places little known to Western science.

The most famous naturalist to join a British naval expedition was Charles Darwin. The observations he made on his journey aboard the *Beagle* in 1831–36 were to form the basis of his great theory of evolution. The expedition charted the southern coasts of South America and sailed around the world. Darwin was given time for many side trips on land. He examined geologic formations and collected numerous plants, animals, and fossils.

Galápagos finch (Darwin's finch)

GALAPAGOS

Charles Darwin was the first of several scientists to visit the Galápagos Islands west of Ecuador. When Darwin arrived in 1835 he found that half the birds and plants were different from species in other parts of the world. About a third of the shorefish and nearly all the reptiles also differed. These variations helped to suggest to Darwin the theory of evolution set forth in his *Origin of Species* (1859).

Galápagos iguana

Galápagos tortoise

TRUE OR FALSE?

T F

AMAZING SOUTH AMERICA

Tourists are drawn to South America's archaeological sites and natural wonders. The continent's attractions are as distinct as Angel Falls in Venezuela, Iguazú Falls on the Argentina-Brazil border, the teeming Amazon Rainforest (accessible from numerous countries), the Galápagos Islands, and sparkling Lake Titicaca. The most famous archaeological sites include Cuzco, Machu Picchu, and the Nazca Lines in Peru, Tiwanaku in Bolivia, and Ingapirca in Ecuador.

Angel Falls is the highest waterfall in the world. About 20 times higher than Niagara Falls, it plunges 3,212 feet (979 meters) and is about 500 feet (150 meters) wide at its base.

The ancient kingdom of Tiwanaku was a major Indian civilization in the Andes Mountains of South America. The main Tiwanaku ruins are located near the southern shore of Lake Titicaca in what is now Bolivia. Scholars believe that much of the site dates from about AD 200–600, though construction continued until about 1000. Although archaeologists once thought Tiwanaku was mainly a ceremonial site, new finds in the late 20th century revealed that it was a bustling city.

The Amazon River's vast waters are like an inland sea that is home to freshwater dolphins (unlike most of the world's dolphins, which live in ocean water), manatees, river stingrays, piranhas, and myriad other fish species. Reptiles of all sizes are lorded over by water-dwelling anacondas and territorial caimans.

Gateway of the Sun

WHERE IS IT FOUND?

ARGENTINA	ECUADOR
BOLIVIA	PERU
BRAZIL	VENEZUELA

The Nazca Lines are large line drawings that appear to be etched into Earth's surface on the arid Pampa Colorada ("Colored Plain" or "Red Plain"), northwest of the city of Nazca in southern Peru. They extend over an area of nearly 190 square miles (500 square kilometers). The people of the Nazca culture constructed most of the Nazca Lines more than 2,000 years ago. The subjects of the Nazca-made lines are generally plants and animals as well as geometric shapes.

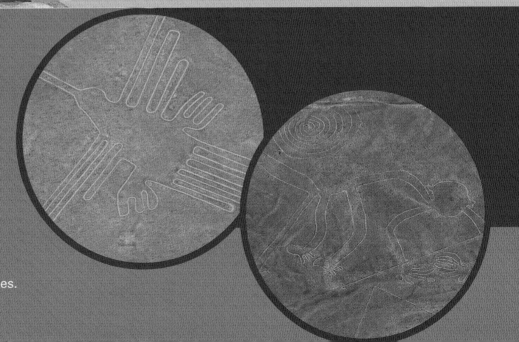

DISCOVER SOUTH AMERICA

RIO DE JANEIRO, BRAZIL

Rio de Janeiro, Brazil, is one of the premier tourist destinations in the world. The city's vibrant culture and many museums, historical sites, and physical features—especially the beaches of Copacabana and Ipanema—attract large crowds of visitors, as do events and festivals such as the annual Carnival and New Year's Eve celebrations.

Christ the Redeemer

Copacabana Beach

CITY ID

BUENOS AIRES, ARGENTINA

Buenos Aires is the capital of Argentina and is one of the largest cities in South America. Buenos Aires has many plazas and parks. Its most important public square is the Plaza de Mayo. There are also many museums and other cultural sites in Buenos Aires.

Casa Rosada ("Pink House")

Plaza de Mayo

Colón Theater

CRUISING THROUGH EUROPE

Many of Europe's great cities were built along its numerous rivers. The major rivers include the Rhine, Seine, and Rhône in the west, the Po in the south, and the Danube, Elbe, Oder, Vistula, Volga, and Don in the center and east. River cruises carry tourists to many top destinations along the Danube, Rhine, and Seine.

Budapest, Hungary

RHINE RIVER

The Rhine River of western Europe flows from the Swiss Alps to the North Sea. The Rhine is about 765 miles (1,230 kilometers) long. No other river in the world has so many old and famous cities on its banks—Basel, Switzerland, Strasbourg, France, and Worms, Mainz, and Cologne, Germany, to name a few. The middle Rhine (between the German cities of Bingen and Bonn), with its rugged scenery and numerous castles, attracts many tourists.

Mäuseturm ("Mouse Tower") near Bingen, Germany

Bratislava, Slovakia

Saint Stephen's Cathedral is one of the most famous landmarks in Vienna, Austria.

Cologne Cathedral

SEINE RIVER

The Seine is the second longest river in France. The Seine begins 18 miles (30 kilometers) northwest of the city of Dijon. From there it flows for 485 miles (780 kilometers) in a northwesterly direction. It empties into the English Channel at Le Havre.

DID YOU KNOW? BUDAPEST WAS FORMED BY THE MERGER OF BUDA, ON THE WEST BANK OF THE DANUBE RIVER, AND PEST, ON THE EAST BANK.

RIVER TRIVIA

DANUBE
RHINE
SEINE
THAMES
VOLGA

Boat trips on the Seine are a popular way to tour Paris, France.

DANUBE RIVER

The most important river of central and southeastern Europe is the Danube. The Danube River starts in the mountains of western Germany and flows for some 1,770 miles (2,850 kilometers) to the Black Sea. The second longest river in Europe, the Danube passes through nine countries: Germany, Austria, Slovakia, Hungary, Croatia, Serbia, Bulgaria, Romania, and Ukraine. Many of the castles and fortresses along the banks, which once protected great empires, now draw tourists to the area.

EXTRAORDINARY EUROPE

European countries are consistently among the top tourist destinations of the world. They draw visitors from within Europe as well as from other continents.

The Arc de Triomphe (in full, Arc de Triomphe de l'Étoile) is 164 feet (50 meters) high and 148 feet (45 meters) wide.

Tivoli Gardens

The Italian city of Pisa is home to the famous bell tower called the Leaning Tower of Pisa. This medieval structure is known for the way it settled, which caused it to lean about 15 feet (4.5 meters) from perpendicular in the late 20th century. Work subsequently done ultimately reduced its lean to about 13.5 feet (4.1 meters). The bell tower, begun in 1173, was meant to stand 185 feet (56 meters) high and was constructed of white marble.

State Hermitage Museum

FIND IT!

One of the most famous clocks in the world is known as Big Ben.

Ávila (in full, Ávila de los Caballeros)

Charles Bridge (Karlův Most)

NUMBER GAME

148
393
8,202
31
185

WONDERS OF THE WORLD

In the ancient world there were seven great man-made structures for travelers to see on a world tour. Lists of the seven wonders sometimes varied. One commonly used list, dating from about the 6th century AD, included the following: the Pyramids of Giza, the Hanging Gardens of Babylon, the statue of Zeus at Olympia, the Temple of Artemis at Ephesus, the Mausoleum at Halicarnassus, the Colossus of Rhodes, and the Pharos of Alexandria.

PYRAMIDS OF GIZA

The Great Pyramid, built for Khufu

Pyramid of Khafre

FIND IT!

The great Pyramids of Giza, Egypt, still stand. They were built between about 2575 and 2465 BC. The designations of the pyramids—Khufu, Khafre, and Menkaure—correspond to the kings for whom they were built.

Pyramid of Menkaure

WHICH WONDER?

Pharos of Alexandria

The Pharos of Alexandria, the most famous lighthouse of the ancient world, was completed during the reign of Ptolemy II of Egypt in about 280 BC. It was a technological triumph and is the archetype of all lighthouses since. The lighthouse stood on the island of Pharos in the harbor of Alexandria and is said to have been more than 350 feet (110 meters) high.

WHO BUILT THE HANGING GARDENS OF BABYLON?

HANGING GARDENS OF BABYLON

The Hanging Gardens of Babylon have long since disappeared. It is not known exactly where they were located or what form they took. According to one theory, great terraces of masonry were built one on top of the other. On these were planted gardens of tropical flowers and trees and avenues of palms, which were irrigated by water pumped from the Euphrates River. Other researchers have proposed that the Hanging Gardens were rooftop gardens. Research in the late 20th and early 21st centuries indicated that the gardens were laid out on a slope designed to imitate a natural mountain landscape.

MAUSOLEUM AT HALICARNASSUS

The Mausoleum at Halicarnassus, in Asia Minor, derived its name from King Mausolus of Caria. After his death in the middle of the 4th century BC, his queen, Artemisia, employed Greek architects to construct a superb monument over his remains. An earthquake between the 11th and the 15th century AD probably destroyed the Mausoleum at Halicarnassus.

TEMPLE OF ARTEMIS AT EPHESUS

Greek colonists at Ephesus, in Asia Minor, built the famous Temple of Artemis. The early Greek settlers found the area's inhabitants worshiping a nature goddess whom the settlers identified with their Artemis (called Diana by the Romans). The Greeks raised a shrine to her, which was rebuilt and enlarged from time to time. The fourth temple, built by the Lydian king Croesus, was the one regarded as the wonder of the world. It was renowned for its great artworks as well as its large size—more than 350 by 180 feet (about 110 by 55 meters).

Remains of the Temple of Artemis at Ephesus in Turkey

COLOSSUS OF RHODES

The Colossus of Rhodes was a great bronze statue, built about 280 BC by the citizens of Rhodes, capital of the Greek island of the same name. It represented the sun god Helios and was said to be 105 feet (32 meters) high. An earthquake toppled the statue in about 225 BC, but its huge fragments were regarded with wonder.

STATUE OF ZEUS AT OLYMPIA

The great sculptor Phidias made the statue of Zeus at Olympia, in the Peloponnesus of Greece, in the 5th century BC. It was a towering structure of ivory and gold, almost 40 feet (12 meters) high, majestic and beautiful. After about nine centuries of existence, the statue was destroyed.

EXPLORATION OF ASIA

BUDDHIST PILGRIMAGES TO INDIA

Xuanzang

Chinese knowledge of India was expanded by the voyages of Chinese Buddhist monks to study there, in the "Holy Land" of Buddhism. The first known Chinese monk to undertake such a pilgrimage was Faxian. He set out in AD 399 in order to bring back Buddhist texts from India that were unavailable in China. After Faxian, many other Chinese monks went on pilgrimages to India. Among them was Xuanzang in the 7th century.

ZHANG QIAN AND THE SILK ROAD

Chinese explorer Zhang Qian was the first man to bring back a reliable account of the lands of Central Asia to the court of China. Han dynasty emperor Wudi dispatched him in 138 BC to establish relations with the Yuezhi people, a Central Asian group. Captured by the Xiongnu, nomadic enemies of China, he was detained for 10 years. Nevertheless, he managed to reach his destination and returned to China after 13 years. Zhang made important diplomatic contacts and collected useful information. In addition to traveling himself, he sent his assistant to visit parts of what are now Uzbekistan and Afghanistan. His missions opened the way for exchanges of envoys between these Central Asian states and China and also brought the Chinese into contact with the outposts of Greek culture established by Alexander the Great.

ZHENG HE SAILS THE INDIAN OCEAN

Zheng He

The greatest Chinese naval explorer was probably the admiral and diplomat Zheng He. His seven major expeditions in the early 15th century helped to extend Chinese maritime and commercial influence throughout the regions bordering the Indian Ocean.

MARCO POLO'S TRAVELS IN ASIA

In 1271 Marco Polo accompanied his father and uncle to Asia. From Venice the Polos sailed to Acre (now 'Akko, Israel). Then the Polos crossed the deserts of Persia (Iran) and Afghanistan. They mounted the heights of the Pamir Mountains, descending to the trading city of Kashgar (Kashi). In central Asia they followed a trail called the Silk Road. In 1275 the Polos reached Shangdu, in Mongolia. This was the summer home of Kublai Khan, the Mongol emperor of China. Kublai sent Marco on many missions to far places in the empire, including Hangzhou, Yunnan, and perhaps also what is now Myanmar. For their return trip to Venice, the Polos took 14 of Kublai Khan's ships. They arrived in Venice in 1295.

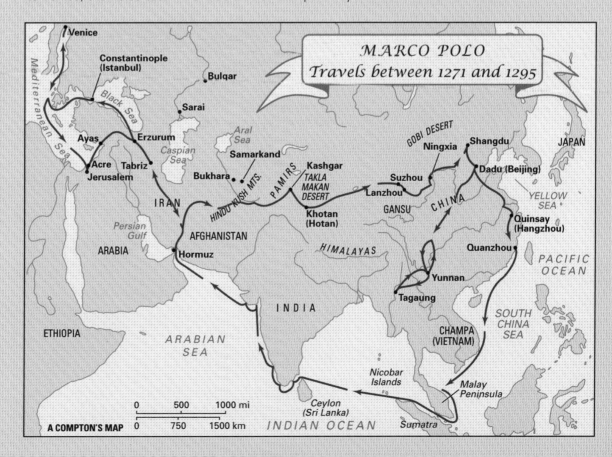

MARCO POLO
Travels between 1271 and 1295

A COMPTON'S MAP

EXPLORING ASIA'S HIGHEST PEAKS

The highest mountains on Earth are found in the Himalayas. This great mountain system of southern Asia stretches for about 1,550 miles (2,500 kilometers) from west to east. Many peaks rise to heights greater than 24,000 feet (7,300 meters), including Mount Everest, Kanchenjunga, Makalu, and Dhaulagiri.

CLIMBING MOUNT EVEREST

Since the early 20th century, numerous mountaineers have undertaken the great challenge of climbing Mount Everest. Many have died trying. Everest is difficult to get to and more difficult to climb, even with modern equipment.

K2

K2, also known as Mount Godwin Austen and as Dapsang, is Earth's second highest mountain. K2 was long considered unclimbable because of its great height, almost unbroken slopes of rock and ice, and precipitous overhangs. The first of several unsuccessful attempts to reach K2's summit was made in 1902. Two members of an Italian party finally reached the summit in July 1954.

MAKALU

Makalu has a height of 27,766 feet (8,463 meters). It is located 14 miles (23 kilometers) east-southeast of Mount Everest. Climbers of Mount Everest had observed Makalu, but attempts to ascend its steep, glacier-covered sides did not begin until 1954. On May 15, 1955, two members—Jean Couzy and Lionel Terray—of a French party reached the summit, and seven more arrived within two days.

At 28,251 feet (8,611 meters) high, K2 is Earth's second highest mountain.

HILLARY AND NORGAY

Several teams tried to climb Everest between 1933 and 1952. A British expedition led by Colonel John Hunt finally succeeded in 1953. At 11:30 a.m. on May 29, 1953, New Zealand mountaineer Edmund Hillary and Tibetan porter Tenzing Norgay reached the 29,035-foot (8,850-meter) summit of Mount Everest. They were the first people to make it to the top of the world's highest mountain.

NANGA PARBAT

Nanga Parbat, also called Diamir, is 26,660 feet (8,126 meters) high, situated in the western Himalayas. The British Alpine climber Albert F. Mummery led the first attempt to ascend the mountain in 1895, but he died in the attempt. At least 30 more climbers also perished on Nanga Parbat because of the severe weather conditions and frequent avalanches. Austrian climber Hermann Buhl finally reached the top in 1953.

LHOTSE

At 27,940 feet (8,516 meters) high, Lhotse is one of the world's highest mountains. Lhotse consists of three Himalayan summits on the Nepalese-Tibetan border just south of Mount Everest. On May 18, 1956, Fritz Luchsinger and Ernest Reiss, two Swiss climbers, made the first ascent of the mountain.

HIMALAYAN HEIGHTS

27,766
29,035
28,169
26,660
27,940

SILK ROAD

The Silk Road was a major thoroughfare for trade and travel between Asia, the Middle East, and Europe. Traders and travelers began using the Silk Road more than 2,000 years ago. Though mainly a trade route, the road was also used by conquering armies, Buddhist missionaries traveling from India to China, and Muslim clerics from the Middle East. Inventions, works of literature, and languages likewise followed its path. When the intrepid Marco Polo traveled from Venice to Cathay (northern China) via the road in the 1270s, it was already 1,500 years old.

THE ROUTE

The Silk Road stretched from east to west for about 4,000 miles (6,400 kilometers). It began at Xi'an, in eastern China. It followed part of the Great Wall of China and passed through the desert in western China. Several different branches then crossed Central Asia. In what is now Pakistan, the Silk Road met up with the Great Royal Road, which came north from India. The route then continued west to the Middle East. From there, goods were shipped across the Mediterranean Sea.

Ruins of the ancient city of Jiaohe in the Uygur Autonomous Region of Xinjiang, western China

FIND IT!

WHO WAS CALLED THE
"FATHER OF THE SILK ROAD"?

- •MARCO POLO
- •ZHANG QIAN

TRADE ALONG THE ROUTE

Caravans transported goods between many cultures along the Silk Road. The caravans were groups of people and animals, such as camels, which carried the goods. Few people traveled the entire route. Different groups carried goods in stages. Silk and other Chinese goods went west, all the way to ancient Rome. Wool, gold, and glass were some of the goods that went east.

THE END OF THE ROAD

By AD 1000 travel on the Silk Road had grown less safe, and traffic had declined. The Mongol Empire revived the route for a while in the 1200s and 1300s. During that time the Italian Marco Polo followed the Silk Road east into China. But in the late 1400s, trade routes between the East and the West moved from land to sea. The Silk Road was abandoned. The search for new trade routes, however, led to a major period of exploration and discovery throughout the world.

Samarkand, Uzbekistan

Ming fortress near Jiuquan, Gansu province, western China

Bukhara, Uzbekistan

Big Wild Goose Pagoda, Xi'an, China

Pamirs region at the far western edge of the Uygur Autonomous Region of Xinjiang, western China

TRANS-SIBERIAN RAILROAD

Siberia is a vast expanse of land that stretches across Russia from the Ural Mountains in the west to the Pacific Ocean in the east. In the 19th century Siberia was Russia's frontier—thinly populated, largely unexplored, yet possessing vast economic potential. Settlement in the region remained sparse until the building of the Trans-Siberian Railroad, which made large-scale immigration possible.

Building the railroad was a great feat of engineering because of the very difficult terrain and extremes of temperature—Siberia can be one of the coldest places in the world. The Siberian section of the line, running from Chelyabinsk in the west to Vladivostok on the Pacific, is about 4,400 miles (7,000 kilometers) long.

Construction of the Trans-Siberian Railroad began in 1891. Work started at the same time from both the eastern and western terminals. The plan originally called for an all-Russian road, but a treaty with China in 1896 enabled the Russians to construct an 800-mile (1,300-kilometer) line through Manchuria, thus shortening the distance to Vladivostok. After Manchuria passed to Japanese hands following the Russo-Japanese War of 1904–05, the Russians proceeded with a longer railway entirely on their own territory.

DID YOU KNOW?

The Trans-Siberian Railroad is the longest single rail system in Russia, stretching from Moscow 5,778 miles (9,198 kilometers) east to Vladivostok or (beyond Vladivostok) 5,867 miles (9,441 kilometers) to the port station of Nakhodka.

NAME IT!

TRANS-SIBERIAN-RAILWAY

——————— Trans-Siberian
——————— Baikal-Amur Mainline
——————— Trans-Manchurian
——————— Trans-Mongolian

THE KREMLIN, MOSCOW

ALONG THE RAIL ROUTE

KHABAROVSK

VLADIVOSTOK

NOVOSIBIRSK OPERA AND BALLET THEATER, NOVOSIBIRSK

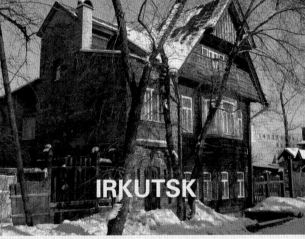

IRKUTSK

SOUTH URAL STATE UNIVERSITY, CHELYABINSK

KRASNOYARSK

AMAZING ASIA

POTALA PALACE

The Potala Palace is a group of religious and administrative buildings in Lhasa, the capital of the Tibet Autonomous Region, in southwestern China. The palace is sacred in Tibetan Buddhism and once served as the seat of the government of Tibet. It was long the home of the Dalai Lama, who was the spiritual and political leader of Tibet.

GREAT STUPA

SANCHI

On a flat-topped sandstone hill that rises some 300 feet (90 meters) above the surrounding country stands India's best-preserved group of Buddhist monuments. Most noteworthy among them is the Great Stupa.

HOW HIGH?

Touch a building name on the left. Then touch the building's height on the right.

MAKKAH ROYAL CLOCK TOWER	1,483 FEET (452 METERS)
PETRONAS TWIN TOWERS	1,614 FEET (492 METERS)
SHANGHAI WORLD FINANCIAL CENTER	2,080 FEET (634 METERS)
TAIPEI 101	1,972 FEET (601 METERS)
TOKYO SKYTREE	1,667 FEET (508 METERS)

KINKAKU TEMPLE

ASIA'S SKYSCRAPERS

TOKYO SKYTREE

PETRONAS TWIN TOWERS

ABRĀJ AL-BAYT

Abrāj al-Bayt, also called Makkah Royal Clock Tower, is a multitowered skyscraper complex adjacent to the Great Mosque in Mecca, Saudi Arabia. Completed in 2012, it is the world's second tallest building. The central clock tower, including its spire, rises to a height of 1,972 feet (601 meters).

TAIPEI 101

SHANGHAI WORLD FINANCIAL CENTER

Approximately two million Muslim pilgrims come to Mecca each year. The city also receives millions of business travelers and tourists yearly.

DISCOVER ASIA

AYUTTHAYA

Ayutthaya, Thailand, is the site of immense temples and other structures that are important both historically and architecturally. Ramathibodi I founded the town in about 1350. Often referred to as Krung Kao ("ancient capital"), the town flourished for more than 400 years. Most of the architecture, art, and literature of Ayutthaya was destroyed in the sack of the city by the armies of the Myanmar king Hsinbyushin in 1767, marking the end of the kingdom.

TIANANMEN SQUARE

The focal point of modern Beijing is Tiananmen Square, a huge plaza that covers nearly 100 acres (40 hectares). On the east Tiananmen Square faces the National Museum of China, a large historical museum. Lying on the western side of the square is the Great Hall of the People. It is the site of the annual meetings of the National People's Congress and contains a meeting hall with more than 10,000 seats.

QIN TOMB

The burial place of the ancient Chinese emperor Shihuangdi, the founder of the Qin dynasty, is known as the Qin tomb. Shihuangdi created the first unified Chinese empire and began the construction of the Great Wall of China. Before his death in 210 BC, he had an enormous tomb complex built. It occupies about 20 square miles (50 square kilometers). Today the Qin tomb is a major archaeological site, famous for its thousands of life-size statues of soldiers.

ELLORA CAVES

Located close to the village of Ellora in western India is a series of 34 magnificent rock-cut temples. The temples were cut from basaltic cliffs.

Tokyo Imperial Palace

PHOTO FIND

EXPLORATION OF AFRICA

IBN BATTUTAH

Ibn Battutah, a great medieval Arab traveler, visited many parts of Africa on his long and numerous journeys. On his pilgrimage to Mecca in 1325–27, he traveled across northern Africa to Egypt. On his second voyage, Ibn Battutah sailed along the east coast of Africa as far as Kilwa, in what is now Tanzania. After traveling extensively in Asia, his final voyage took him across the Sahara to western Africa. He spent a year in the Mali empire, then at the height of its power. In all, he traveled some 75,000 miles (more than 120,000 kilometers).

IBN BATTUTAH DESCRIBED HIS EXPERIENCES IN A FAMOUS TRAVEL BOOK CALLED THE *RIHLAH (TRAVELS)*.

THE PORTUGUESE EXPLORE AFRICA

The Portuguese dreamed of finding an all-water route around Africa. Prince Henry, who had sent ships on voyages down the African coast, laid the groundwork. Exploration continued under his nephew, King John II. In 1482 John sent the navigator Diogo Cão to search for a seaway around southern Africa to India. Cão instead discovered the mouth of the Congo River. In 1487 Bartolomeu Dias took over the task of finding the southern end of Africa. In an impressive feat of navigation, Dias rounded the stormy Cape of Good Hope at Africa's southern tip in 1488. In 1497–99 the Portuguese navigator Vasco da Gama made the first trip around the Cape of Good Hope to India.

EXPLORER ID

IBN BATTUTAH

JOHANNES REBMANN

DAVID LIVINGSTONE

JOHN SPEKE

BARTOLOMEU DIAS

MUNGO PARK

BARTOLOMEU DIAS · 1450–1500

David Livingstone.

DAVID LIVINGSTONE'S CAREER CAN BE DIVIDED INTO FOUR STAGES. TOUCH EACH STAGE TO HEAR MORE.

EARLY JOURNEYS (1841–51)
CROSSING THE CONTINENT (1853–56)
ZAMBEZI EXPEDITION (1858–64)
QUEST FOR THE NILE (1866–73)

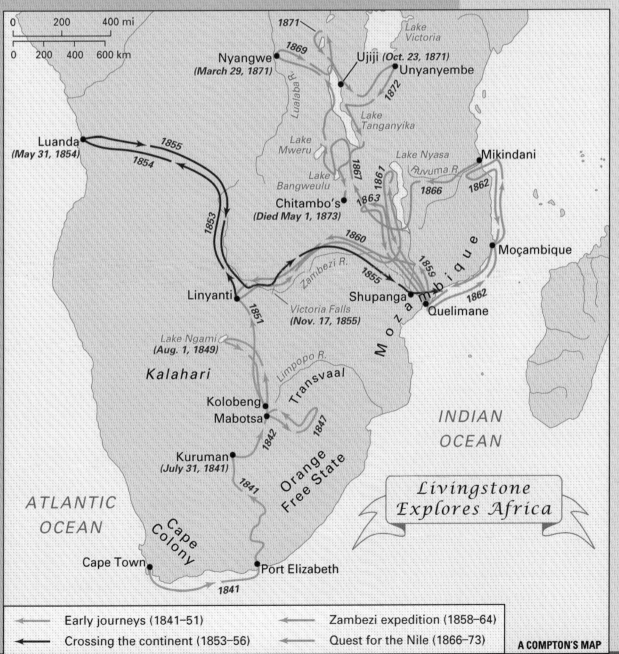

0 200 400 mi	
0 200 400 600 km	

1871
1869
Nyangwe (March 29, 1871)
Ujiji (Oct. 23, 1871)
Unyanyembe
Lake Victoria
1872
Lualaba R.
Lake Tanganyika
Luanda (May 31, 1854)
1855
1854
Lake Mweru
Lake Nyasa
Mikindani
Ruvuma R.
1867
1861
1866
1862
Lake Bangweulu
1863
Chitambo's (Died May 1, 1873)
1853
1860
1859
Moçambique
1855
Zambezi R.
Linyanti
1855
Shupanga
1862
Quelimane
1851
Victoria Falls (Nov. 17, 1855)
Lake Ngami (Aug. 1, 1849)
Limpopo R.
Kalahari
Transvaal
Kolobeng
Mabotsa
1842
1847
INDIAN OCEAN
Kuruman (July 31, 1841)
Orange Free State
1841
ATLANTIC OCEAN
Cape Colony
Mozambique
Livingstone Explores Africa
Cape Town
Port Elizabeth
1841

Livingstone Explores Africa

→ Early journeys (1841–51)	→ Zambezi expedition (1858–64)
→ Crossing the continent (1853–56)	→ Quest for the Nile (1866–73)

A COMPTON'S MAP

ASTONISHING AFRICA

Table Mountain

Table Mountain is a flat-topped mountain in southwestern South Africa, overlooking Cape Town and Table Bay. The distinctive-looking mountain is one of Cape Town's most recognized landmarks and is a popular tourist attraction that offers hiking, camping, and other activities.

CITIES GAME

THE NAME CASABLANCA MEANS "WHITE HOUSE" IN SPANISH.

Gonder

Hassan II Mosque, Casablanca, Morocco

DISCOVER AFRICA

JAMAA EL-FNA SQUARE

BAB AGNAOU

MARRAKECH

Marrakech was the first of Morocco's four imperial cities. The ancient section of the city, known as the medina, was designated a World Heritage site in 1985. The medina in Marrakech is called the "red city" because of its buildings and walls of beaten clay.

WHICH COUNTRY?

EGYPT

MOROCCO

SOUTH AFRICA

SENEGAL

WHAT DO YOU KNOW? YES NO

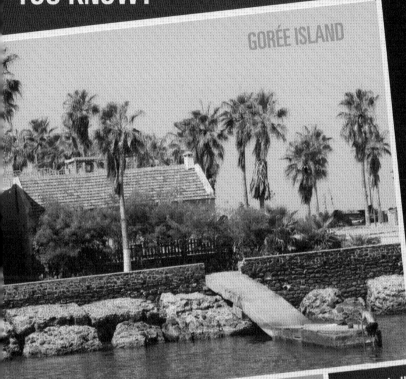

GORÉE ISLAND

MAISON DES ESCLAVES ("SLAVE HOUSE")

VALLEY OF THE KINGS

Just west of the Nile River in Upper Egypt is the Valley of the Kings. It was part of the ancient city of Thebes and was the burial site of almost all the kings (pharaohs) of the 18th, 19th, and 20th dynasties (1539–1075 BC). The longest tomb (number 20) belongs to Queen Hatshepsut (reigned c. 1472–58 BC), whose burial chamber is nearly 700 feet (215 meters) from the entrance and descends 320 feet (100 meters) into the rock.

Hot air balloons are one way to tour the Valley of the Kings.

DID ROBBEN ISLAND ALWAYS HOUSE A PRISON?

PRISON ON ROBBEN ISLAND

ROBBEN ISLAND

Robben Island, off the coast of Cape Town, South Africa, is the site of a famous apartheid-era prison. From 1964 to 1982 Nelson Mandela was incarcerated at Robben Island Prison. After his release, Mandela helped end the country's **apartheid** system.

AFRICA'S PROTECTED AREAS

SERENGETI NATIONAL PARK

Country: Tanzania
Established: 1951
Area: 5,700 square miles
(14,763 square kilometers)
Features: Huge herds of animals, especially wildebeests, zebras, and gazelles, range over the land. The Serengeti is also home to about 3,000 lions and large numbers of elephants, spotted hyenas, leopards, rhinoceroses, hippopotamuses, giraffes, cheetahs, baboons, and crocodiles. More than 350 species of birds, including owls, eagles, and flamingos, have been recorded.

DID YOU KNOW?

Serengeti National Park is the only place in Africa where massive animal migrations still take place.

KRUGER NATIONAL PARK

Country: South Africa
Established: 1898
Area: 7,523 square miles
(19,485 square kilometers)
Features: Kruger National Park is the largest national park in South Africa. Many different insects, birds, reptiles, and amphibians make the park their home. There are also more than 100 species of mammals.

AFRICAN ANIMALS QUIZ

Spotted hyenas

Elephant

PARK ID

Wildebeest (gnu)

Serengeti is home to some 3,000 lions.

THE LION IS THE SECOND LARGEST MEMBER OF THE CAT FAMILY. DO YOU KNOW THE LARGEST **?**

The "Big Five" mammals attract many visitors to Kruger National Park. Can you name the "Big Five" mammals?

ETOSHA NATIONAL PARK

Country: Namibia
Established: 1907
Area: 8,598 square miles
(22,269 square kilometers)
Features: The park centers on the Etosha Pan, a vast expanse of salt with lone salt springs, used by animals as salt licks. It has one of the largest populations of big-game species in the world, including lions, elephants, rhinoceroses, elands, zebras, and springbok. Abundant birdlife includes flamingos, vultures, hawks, eagles, ostriches, guinea fowl, and geese.

VIRUNGA NATIONAL PARK

Country: Democratic Republic of the Congo (DRC)
Established: 1925
Area: 3,050 square miles
(7,900 square kilometers)
Features: Elevations, climates, and habitats vary notably in Virunga National Park. The park encompasses mountains, savannas, peat bogs, marshes, lava plains, eastern steppe vegetation, and various types of forests, including tropical rainforest and bamboo. The park is home to abundant wildlife, including elephants, whose numbers decreased in the late 20th century, and lions, which have increased in number, unlike most other large mammals. Hippopotamuses, rare mountain gorillas, okapis, antelope, warthogs, and pelicans all live in Virunga as well.

MOUNTAIN ZEBRA NATIONAL PARK

Country: South Africa
Established: 1937
Area: 108 square miles (280 square kilometers)
Features: Mountain Zebra National Park was founded primarily to protect the diminishing mountain zebra, which are shorter and stockier than the common zebra. The park also supports black wildebeests, elands, and several other species of antelopes.

DID YOU KNOW?

Zebra stripes are like fingerprints.
No two zebras are alike.

Springbok

Guinea fowl

Mountain gorilla in Virunga National Park, DRC

Cape mountain zebra at Mountain Zebra National Park, South Africa

EXPLORING AUSTRALIA AND NEW ZEALAND

TASMAN FINDS TASMANIA AND NEW ZEALAND

Dutch navigator and explorer Abel Tasman was the first European to reach the Australian island that was later named Tasmania in his honor. In the early 1640s the Dutch East India Company chose Tasman to explore the southern Pacific and Indian oceans. Tasman set sail in August 1642 from what is now Jakarta, Indonesia. After sailing to the island of Mauritius, he saw a large island that he named Van Diemen's Land (now Tasmania). He also "discovered" New Zealand, Tonga, and the Fiji Islands.

DID YOU KNOW?
The Abel Tasman National Park is located on the South Island of New Zealand.

THE VOYAGES OF JAMES COOK

CAPTAIN COOK
LANDED HERE
28TH APRIL, A.D. 1770.
THIS MONUMENT
WAS ERECTED A.D. 1870,
BY THE HONORABLE THOMAS HOLT, M.L.C
VICTORIA REGINA THE EARL OF BELMORE, GOVERNOR, &C

British explorer James Cook led three wide-ranging expeditions to the Pacific. Cook surveyed a greater length of coastline than any other man and remade the map of the Pacific. He also claimed New Zealand and eastern Australia for Britain. Cook named the east coast of Australia New South Wales because he thought it resembled the south coast of Wales in Britain.

A NEW PENAL COLONY

Not long after James Cook claimed eastern Australia for Britain, the first British settlers began arriving. The British government decided to colonize New South Wales by setting up an overseas penal (prison) settlement. Convicts would be "transported" to eastern Australia to serve their sentences—so far from home they could never hope to return.

CROSSING THE CONTINENT

In 1860 the only part of Australia that had been well explored was the coastline. The inner portion, or Outback, was almost completely unknown except to the Australian Aborigines who lived there. Starting in 1860 two rival expeditions backed by two different colonies raced to be the first to cross the continent from south to north.

BURKE&WILLS 150 YEARS CROSSING AUSTRALIA 2010
AUSTRALIA 60c

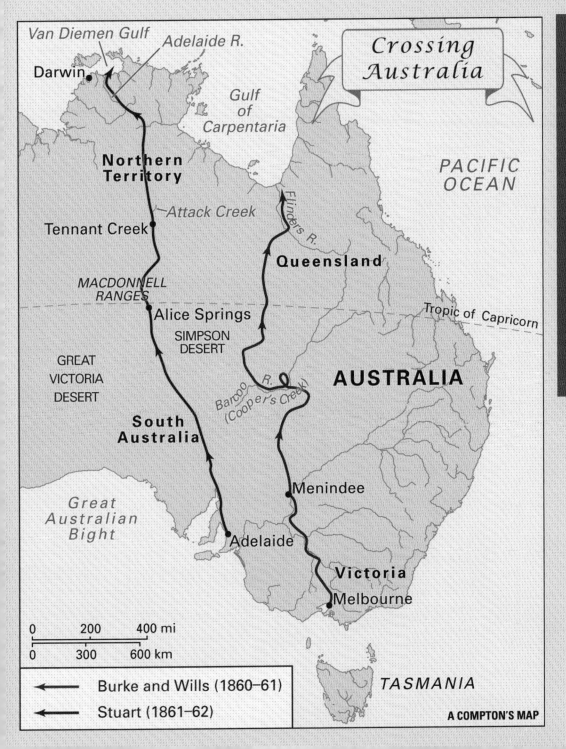

Crossing Australia

Van Diemen Gulf
Adelaide R.
Darwin
Gulf of Carpentaria
Northern Territory
PACIFIC OCEAN
Attack Creek
Flinders R.
Tennant Creek
Queensland
MACDONNELL RANGES
Alice Springs
Tropic of Capricorn
SIMPSON DESERT
GREAT VICTORIA DESERT
Barcoo R. (Cooper's Creek)
AUSTRALIA
South Australia
Great Australian Bight
Menindee
Adelaide
Victoria
Melbourne

0   200   400 mi
0   300   600 km

⟵ Burke and Wills (1860–61)
⟵ Stuart (1861–62)

TASMANIA

A COMPTON'S MAP

TRUE OR FALSE?

T
F

AMAZING AUSTRALIA AND OCEANIA

DESTINATION CITIES

Wellington, New Zealand

Brisbane, Australia

Port Arthur

Sydney Tower

Melbourne, Australia

DID YOU KNOW?

Several million tourists travel to Sydney annually.

Sydney Harbour

Fiji

Fiordland National Park

About one-third of New Zealand's land area is devoted to national parks, wilderness areas, and other conservation efforts. There are 14 national parks, of which Fiordland is the largest.

Twelve Apostles

BRISBANE
MELBOURNE
SYDNEY
WELLINGTON

EXPLORING POLAR REGIONS

The North and South poles are the coldest and most remote regions on Earth. For hundreds of years these icy areas at each end of the globe have challenged explorers. Many brave people have risked their lives investigating the Arctic and the Antarctic.

RACE FOR THE NORTH POLE

In 1909 American explorer Robert E. Peary claimed to be the first to reach the North Pole. Years later, American explorer Richard E. Byrd claimed that he reached the pole by airplane on May 9, 1926. However, some experts later doubted that either Peary or Byrd actually made it to the North Pole. Days after Byrd's flight, it was confirmed that Norwegian explorer Roald Amundsen and two companions, Lincoln Ellsworth and Umberto Nobile, had flown over the North Pole.

ROBERT E. PEARY

EXPLORING ANTARCTICA

	ROALD AMUNDSEN 1910–12	RICHARD E. BYRD 1928–30
NATHAN PALMER 1820	ROBERT F. SCOTT 1910–12	VIVIAN FUCHS 1957–58

POLAR EXPLORERS QUIZ

Touch an explorer's name on the left. Then touch what that explorer is known for on the right.

	FIRST TO FLY OVER THE SOUTH POLE	FIRST TO REACH THE SOUTH POLE	LED FIRST OVERLAND CROSSING OF ANTARCTICA	FIRST TO REACH THE NORTH POLE
ROALD AMUNDSEN				
ROBERT E. PEARY				
VIVIAN FUCHS				
RICHARD E. BYRD				

EXPLORERS' ROUTES
- Palmer 1820
- Amundsen 1910–12
- Scott 1910–12
- Byrd 1928–30
- Fuchs 1957–58

By ship — By airplane — By sledge — By snow tractor

A COMPTON'S MAP

WHEN DID IT HAPPEN?

1911

1958

1926

1986

1905

TOURISTS IN ANTARCTICA

TERRA NOVA EXPEDITION

British naval officer and explorer Robert F. Scott led the Terra Nova Expedition to the South Pole. The expedition sailed for Antarctica in 1910. Equipped with motor sledges, ponies, and dogs, Scott and 11 others started overland for the South Pole on October 24, 1911. The motors soon broke down, the ponies had to be shot, and the dog teams were sent back. The men continued by hauling their own heavy sledges. By December 31 seven men had been sent back to the base camp on Ross Island. Scott and the remaining four men—Edward Wilson, H.R. Bowers, Lawrence Oates, and Edgar Evans—reached the South Pole in mid-January 1912, only to find that Roald Amundsen had already been there the previous month.

SPACE TRAVEL

On April 12, 1961, Soviet cosmonaut Yury Gagarin became the first human being to travel in space. He orbited Earth aboard the Vostok 1 spacecraft. Within less than 10 years of Gagarin's voyage, U.S. astronaut Neil Armstrong became the first person to set foot on the Moon, on July 20, 1969. The Soviet Union (now Russia) and the United States, engaged in a "space race," were originally the main countries exploring space. Many other countries are now involved.

SPACE RACE	UNITED STATES	SOVIET UNION

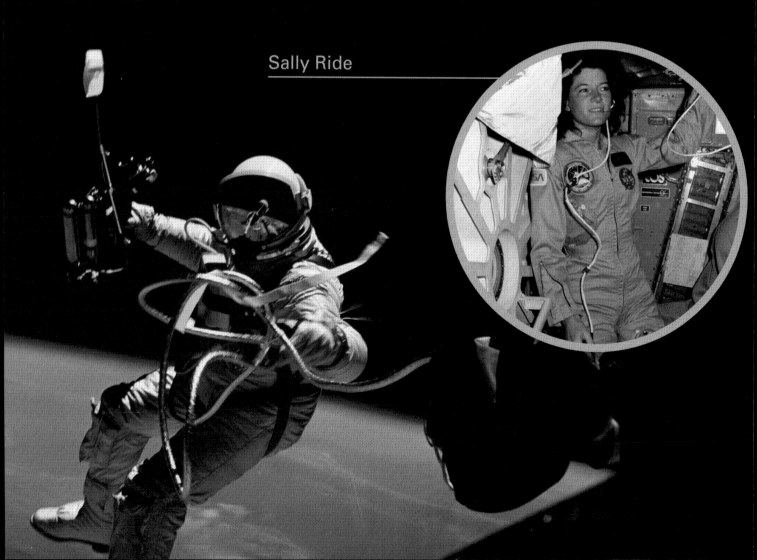

Sally Ride

SPACE SHUTTLES

In 1981 the United States launched the first reusable spacecraft, called a space shuttle, designed to transport people and cargo to and from orbiting spacecraft. The first shuttle missions were successful. But in January 1986 the shuttle *Challenger* exploded 73 seconds after liftoff. Its seven-person crew perished. Among them was a schoolteacher, on board as the first teacher in space. The United States returned to space in September 1988 with the launching of the shuttle *Discovery*. The shuttle program suffered its second fatal disaster in February 2003 when *Columbia* broke up over Texas while returning to Earth, killing all seven crew members. NASA ended the shuttle program in 2011.

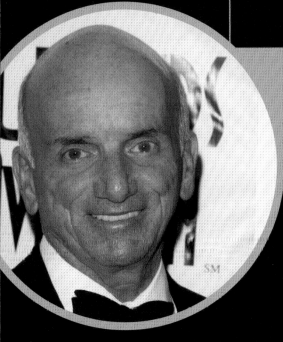

Space tourist Dennis Tito

SPACE TOURISM

Space tourism is recreational space travel, either on established government-owned vehicles such as the Russian Soyuz and the International Space Station (ISS) or on a growing number of vehicles fielded by private companies.

Space shuttle *Atlantis* docked to Mir station

SPACE STATIONS

Space stations are spacecraft that stay in orbit for a long period of time. Scientists can spend days or even months at a station doing experiments. The Soviet Union began launching space stations in 1971, and the United States followed in 1973. The Soviet space station Mir was launched into Earth orbit in 1986 and served as a space laboratory for more than 14 years.

TRAVEL TRIVIA
PHOTO FIND